The Rockwool Foundation Research Unit

Emigration from Poland and the wages for those who stayed behind

Christian Dustmann, Tommaso Frattini
and Anna Rosso

University Press of Southern Denmark
Odense 2012

Emigration from Poland and the wages for those who stayed behind

Published by:
© The Rockwool Foundation Research Unit and University Press of Southern Denmark

Copying from this book is permitted only within institutions that have agreements with CopyDan, and only in accordance with the limitations laid down in the agreement

Address:
The Rockwool Foundation Research Unit
Sølvgade 10, 2nd floor
DK-1307 Copenhagen K

Telephone   +45 33 34 48 00

Fax   +45 33 34 48 99

E-mail   forskningsenheden@rff.dk

Home page   www.rff.dk

ISBN 978-87-90199-72-2

October 2012
Print run: 400
Printed by: Specialtrykkeriet Viborg

Price: 40.00 DKK, including 25% VAT

Contents

1. Introduction 5

2. Background, data and descriptive evidence 6
   2.1 Emigration from Poland 6
   2.2 Data 8
   2.3 Descriptive evidence 9

3. Empirical strategy 13
   3.1 Non-random emigration 15

4. Results 16

5. Discussion and Conclusions 18

References 20

Emigration from Poland and the wages for those who stayed behind[1]

Christian Dustmann,° Tommaso Frattini[§] and Anna Rosso°

°University College London and CReAM
[§]Università degli Studi di Milano, CReAM, LdA and IZA

Non-technical summary of the main research findings of the research report prepared for the Rockwool Foundation

1. Introduction

Over the decade following the late 1990s, Poland experienced a dramatic increase in emigration. Whereas in 1998 the share of emigrants from the overall population was about 0.50%, it had increased to 2.3% only a decade later. There was large regional variation in emigration rates, with the share of emigrants in 2007 ranging between 1% and 5.6% across Poland's 16 provinces. Over the period, emigrants also became increasingly younger and better educated compared to non-emigrants.

These large increases in emigration are likely to have had an impact on the Polish labour market and, in particular, on the wages of those who stayed behind. It is this question that we address in our study, which investigates the wage impact of emigration over a period of 10 years (1998–2007), during which time emigration from Poland was at its highest.

We frame our analysis within a simple theoretical model in which output is produced with a constant returns to scale technology, using capital and different types of labour. Such a model suggests that wage effects should be positive for

---

[1] Financial support from the Rockwool Foundation is gratefully acknowledged. We thank the Foundation's Research Unit for their support, constructive comments, and productive collaboration during the project. We also wish to thank Iga Magda for her invaluable help with the data and Orazio Attanasio, David Card, Ian Preston, Florian Hoffmann, Thomas Lemieux, Uta Schoenberg, and participants to the CReAM-NORFACE Conference "Migration: Economic Change, Social Challenge", and to seminars at the University of British Columbia and the University of Bologna for their constructive comments.

workers in those skill groups whose relative supply is decreased by emigration, and negative for workers in skill groups whose relative supply is increased by emigration. Moreover, if capital is insufficiently mobile in the short run, the effect on average wages can be expected to be positive.

Our empirical results indicate that, overall, emigration had a positive effect on the wages of those who did not emigrate. Between 1998 and 2007 real wages in Poland increased by about 1.7% per year. Emigration may have contributed about 0.18% per year, and thus may have accounted for about 1/10 of the overall real wage growth.

Across skill groups, it was particularly those in the middle of the educational distribution that experienced the largest gains as a result of emigration. The workers with intermediate level education who stayed behind experienced annual wage growth of 1.4%; about 1/6 of their overall real wage growth during this period may have been explained by emigration. The effect on the highly educated was also positive, but smaller, and the result of the calculation is less robust.

The effect on the wages of those with a low level of education was slightly negative, albeit not significantly different from zero in most cases. This result is in line with emigration being more concentrated among individuals in the middle and upper parts of the educational distribution.

Within the simple model that we developed, the results also indicate that the capital stock in Poland did not diminish in line with emigration, which explains the positive overall effect on wages.

2. Background, data and descriptive evidence

2.1 Emigration from Poland

The first large-scale migrations from Poland took place towards the end of the nineteenth century, when sluggish economic development and large population growth led many Poles to seek better opportunities in other countries. The trend intensified during the inter-war period: between 1919 and 1938, about one million people emigrated permanently to the U.S., France and Brazil (Zubrzycki 1953), and circulatory migration took place to Germany and Latvia. Although emigration slowed after the great depression of the 1930s, it increased again in the period after WWII, the emigrants leaving mainly for political reasons. Between 1950 and 1992 more than two million Poles left the country (see Fassmann and Munz 1994), a large proportion of them moving to the United States.

In the decade following the 1989 fall of the Berlin Wall emigration from Poland was quite modest, because of relatively favourable economic conditions in Poland. From about 1998 onwards, however, after a slow-down in GDP growth and a decrease in employment, it began increasing steadily until it peaked in 2007. Figure 1 and Table 1 provide more detailed information about the overall recent emigration trends from Poland based on data from the Polish Labour Force Survey (PLFS).

Figure 1: Total annual numbers of emigrants, 1994-2008, in thousands

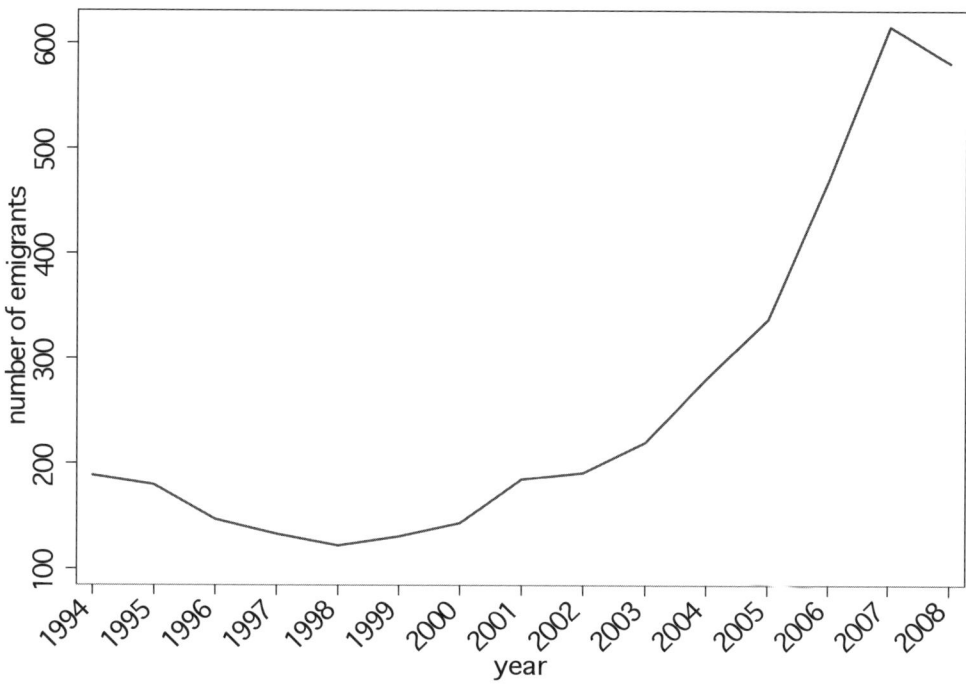

Source: Polish LFS
Note: The chart shows the total stock of Poles residing abroad. The number for each year is an average over the four quarters of that year.

As the figure shows, the stock of emigrants nearly quintupled between 1998 and 2007, from just above 100,000 in 1998 to over 600,000 in 2007, but decreased slightly from 2007 to 2008 because of the global economic crisis, which severely affected the main destination countries.

In 2004, Poland became a member of the European Union, which gave its citizens the right to travel freely across all EU member states. In addition, the UK, Sweden and Ireland allowed Polish citizens full access to their labour markets, while the other EU countries took advantage of a seven-year transition arrangement under which Poles were refused the right to work. This constraint was not strictly imposed by all countries, however; for instance, Germany (on a case-by-case basis) gave many Poles access to its labour market, which led to annual increases in the number of emigrants of between 20% and 40% in the years after 2004 (see Kaczmarczyk and Okólski 2008 and Kaczmarczyk, Mioduszewska, and Zylicz 2009 for details on post-accession Polish emigration).

Table 1: Number of Poles living abroad

	Stock	% Change	Flow	Share of the population (%)
1994	192,472			0.79
1995	185,389	-3.7	-7,083	0.74
1996	153,227	-17.3	-32,162	0.61
1997	139,805	-8.8	-13,422	0.55
1998	127,515	-8.8	-12,290	0.50
1999	133,247	4.5	5,733	0.51
2000	146,656	10.1	13,408	0.56
2001	191,166	30.4	44,511	0.72
2002	199,418	4.3	8,251	0.76
2003	229,833	15.3	30,416	0.87
2004	288,444	25.5	58,610	1.08
2005	343,884	19.2	55,440	1.29
2006	477,664	38.9	133,780	1.77
2007	626,927	31.2	149,263	2.29
2008	590,658	-5.8	-36,269	2.17

Source: Polish LFS

Note: In the first column we report the stock of working age (15-65) emigrants in each year, in the second column the percentage change in the stock with respect to the previous year, and in the third column the flow of emigrants, given by the difference in the stock of the year with the previous year. Column 4 shows the share of emigrants in the total working age (15-65) population.

2.2 Data

The main dataset for our analysis is the Polish Labour Force Survey (PLFS), a rotating quarterly panel of about 15,000 households, or 50,000 individuals per quarter, conducted by the Polish Central Statistical Office (GUS) in all Poland's 16 provinces (*voivodeships*). This survey covers all individuals aged 15 and above who are living in the same household, and each household is interviewed four times: in two initial consecutive quarters and then again in two consecutive quarters after a gap of two quarters. Thus, the entire interview period spans 1.5 years. We focus on the data for the 1998-2007 period, and restrict our analysis to the age group between 15 and 65 years.

The PLFS provides information on demographic, personal and household characteristics of all the individuals interviewed, including age, education, current and past region of residence, country of birth and number of children. It also collects detailed information on the economic activity of each household member during the week preceding the interview, including employment status, work arrangements, occupation, industry and monthly net wages. In addition, and most important for our analysis, it gathers detailed demographic information – age, education level, region of origin, relationship with other household members and country of present residence – for individuals who are part of the household but who have been residing abroad for more than three months. This information allows us to construct a comprehensive measure of out-migration. We use the PLFS data to construct the two key variables for our analysis: (i) emigration rates, by region and time period, and (ii) non-emigrant wages, by region, time period and educational group.

In addition to the PLFS, for some parts of the analysis, we draw on other data for the four main countries of destination for Polish emigrants. We use micro-data for Germany (IAB Employment History Data), the UK (UK Labour Force Survey) and the U.S. (Integrated Public Use Microdata Series of the March Current Population Survey, IPUMS-CPS) and aggregated data for Ireland (based on the Earnings Hours and Employment Costs Survey). In particular, we use these data to cross-check the validity of the emigration measures in the PLFS and to construct our instrumental variables, which are based on wage growth in the destination countries.

2.3 Descriptive evidence

How do emigrants differ from non-emigrants? In Table 2, we report the average characteristics of emigrants and non-emigrants for the years 1998 and 2007.

Table 2: Average age, gender ratio and education in 1998 and 2007

	Total Population		Emigrants	
	1998	2007	1998	2007
Age	38.1	38.6	34.0	32.3
% females	51%	51%	42%	34%
Education:				
% low	29%	14%	12%	5%
% intermediate	60%	67%	74%	76%
% high	11%	19%	13%	20%
% of 25-40 olds	30%	32%	47%	54%

Source: Polish LFS
Note: Entries are the average age, percentage of females, educational distribution, and the share of individuals aged 25 to 40 for the total population and emigrants in the working age 15-65 for both sexes in 1998 and 2007. People with low-level education are individuals who have at most lower secondary education, or up to 8 years of schooling. People with intermediate-level education are individuals with secondary education, or between 9 and 13 years of schooling. People with high-level education are individuals with post-secondary or tertiary education, or more than 13 years of schooling.

The figures in the table show that emigrants in both years are substantially younger than non-emigrants, with the average age for emigrants decreasing by about 2 years between 1998 and 2007. When education level is defined as low, intermediate or high on the basis of individual qualifications, emigrants are also found to be far better educated.[2] For both 1998 and 2007, the fraction of individuals with a low level of education is smaller in the population of emigrants, while the fraction of those with an intermediate level of education is larger. The overall share of individuals with a low level of education decreased substantially between 1998 and 2007 for both emigrants and non-emigrants, with the drop being even larger for emigrants. These figures suggest that emigrants are over-represented among the intermediate- and high-education groups but under-represented in the low-education group.

Are these numbers similar for the different regions and across time periods? We answer this question graphically in Figure 2, which (for all years and all regions) plots the share of each education group in the emigrant population against the share of each education group in the overall population.

If the skill composition of the emigrant population were identical to that of the overall population, then all the dots would lie on the 45-degree line. As the figure clearly shows, however, such is not the case: for most region-year pairs, the share of those in the intermediate-education group – and to a lesser extent, those in the high-education group – is higher among emigrants than among the overall population. In contrast, the share of individuals with a low level of education is clearly smaller among emigrants than in the overall population. These numbers suggest that emigration led to a decrease in the share of population with intermediate and high levels of education but to a relative increase in the share of the less educated.

A simple model of the labour market, similar to that derived in Dustmann, Frattini and Preston (2012), suggests that the effect of emigration on wages of a particular skill group is positive if emigrants are more densely represented in that skill group than non-emigrants: as the supply of that type of skill decreases relative to that of other skill groups, so their wages increase. Conversely, the effect will be negative for those skill groups where emigration leads to an increase in relative supply. Finally, emigration will have a positive effect on average wages if capital is not perfectly mobile (at least in the short term), and thus does not immediately adjust to the decrease in labour supply. The skill composition of Polish emigrants suggests therefore that workers in the intermediate (and high) skill groups will experience wage increase, while workers with low education will possibly face a wage decrease as a result of emigration.

---

2 'Low education' refers to individuals with at most a lower secondary education, or up to 8 years of schooling; 'intermediate education' refers to those with a secondary education, or between 9 and 13 years of schooling, and 'high education' refers to individuals with post-secondary or tertiary education, or more than 13 years of schooling.

Figure 2: Emigrants and total population: shares in each education group

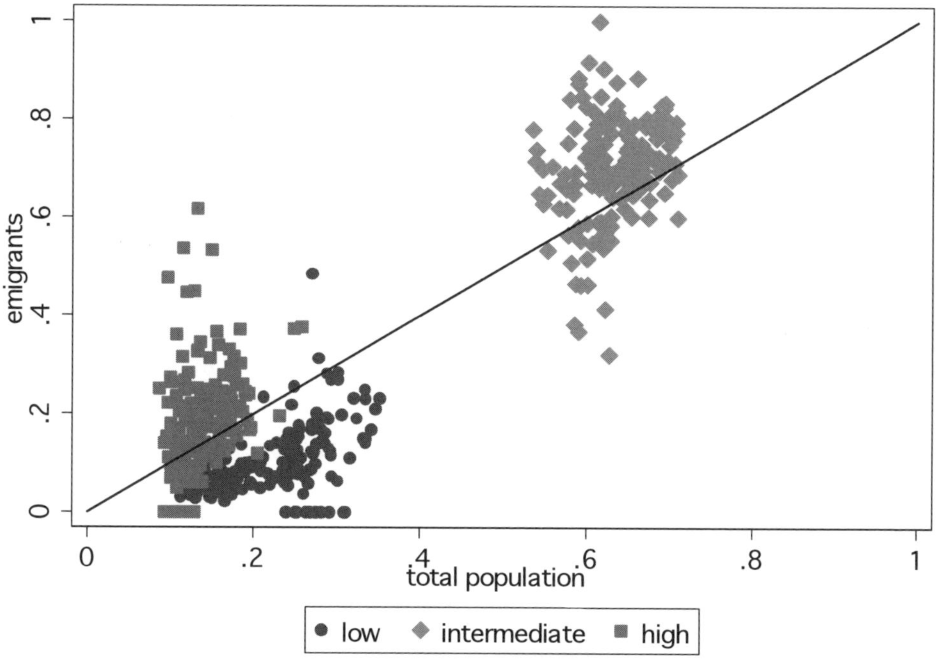

Source: Polish LFS 1998-2007.
Note: The figure plots for each region and year the share of each education group in the total number of working age (15-65) emigrants against the share in the total working-age population.

How, then, are emigrants to the different destination countries selected along the education distribution?

Table 3: Emigrant education by destination country

	% total emigrants	Education			Average age
		low	*Intermediate*	*high*	
Germany					
all emigrants					
1998	27%	11%	78%	11%	33
2007	18%	7%	82%	11%	37
recent emigrants					
1998	36%	11%	77%	12%	32
2007	16%	7%	80%	12%	35

Table 3, continued

	% total emigrants	Education			Average age
		low	Intermediate	high	
UK					
all emigrants					
1998	5%	10%	67%	23%	26
2007	31%	4%	71%	26%	29
recent emigrants					
1998	6%	16%	75%	9%	25
2007	37%	4%	71%	25%	28
USA					
all emigrants					
1998	29%	16%	74%	10%	39
2007	6%	3%	77%	19%	40
recent emigrants					
1998	15%	13%	72%	15%	32
2007	3%	2%	71%	26%	34
Ireland					
all emigrants					
1998	0%	0%	0%	0%	0
2007	12%	2%	72%	26%	30
recent emigrants					
1998	0%	0%	0%	0%	0
2007	12%	2%	70%	28%	29
Europe					
all emigrants					
1998	55%	11%	78%	11%	31
2007	84%	5%	77%	17%	32
recent emigrants					
1998	73%	10%	80%	10%	30
2007	88%	5%	76%	19%	31

Source: Polish LFS
Note: We report the share of all emigrants and the share of recent emigrants (those who emigrated within the previous year) for Germany, UK, USA, Ireland and Europe (EU27) in 1998 and 2007 in the first column. In columns 2-4 we report the distribution of education for those two groups in 1998 and 2007 and in the last column we report the average age in the two groups in 1998 and 2007. Emigrants are of working age (15-65).

In the first column of Table 3, we report the share of Polish emigrants living in Germany, Ireland (there were no Polish emigrants in Ireland in 1998 according to the PLFS), the UK and the U.S., as well as the overall number living in any EU27 country, for the years 1998 and 2007. The table reports figures both for all Polish emigrants and for those who emigrated within the previous year (recent emigrants). In 1998, almost one third of all Polish emigrants lived in the U.S., just under 30% in Germany, and only 5% in the UK. The new flows of emigrants, however, were mostly directed toward Germany (36%), and to a lesser extent the U.S. (15%), with only 6% of new emigrants going to the UK and no emigration to Ireland.

By 2007, in contrast, the situation was reversed: one third of Polish emigrants were now living in the UK, 18% in Germany, 12% in Ireland and only 6% in the U.S. This shift reflects a sharp change in the destination of emigration flows: in 2007, 37% of new Polish emigrants chose the UK as a destination, 12% chose Ireland, 16% chose Germany and only 3% moved to the U.S. In that same year, 88% of the entire population of new Polish emigrants moved to EU countries, which by 2007 accounted for 84% of all Polish emigrants, up from 55% in 1998.

The destination countries do, however, differ greatly in the composition of their Polish immigrant population. In columns (2-4) of Table 3, we report the distribution of immigrants across education groups in each destination country, and in column (5), we show the average age of emigrants in the different countries. Emigrants to Germany and the U.S. are older and less educated (especially those to the U.S.), while emigrants to the UK and Ireland are far younger, with a higher share of those with intermediate or high education. Although the average age of emigrants in the U.S. has remained stable over the years, emigrants to Germany became older, especially compared to the average age of the total emigrant population.

3. Empirical strategy

To estimate the effect of emigration on the wages of stayers, we adopt an empirical approach based on comparisons of wages and emigration rates in different regions, where we regress wages of resident workers in each Polish region on the relative quantity of emigrants in that particular region and appropriate control variables. Our estimating equation, which can be derived from a theoretical model similar to the one developed in Dustmann, Frattini and Preston (2012), has mean wages as the variable to be explained, and it varies over time and over regions. We take account of all factors that vary only across regions or over time, and thus we allow the wage variation to be partly explained by factors and conditions specific to each region and time period (years), i.e. region-specific and year-specific effects respectively. Furthermore, we take account of changes in the age and skill composition of the overall non-emigrant labour force. We detail these variables in Table 4.

Having taken account of all these important contributory factors, we can now isolate the effect of emigration on the wages of skill groups. We define skill groups in terms of education levels, and we construct the following measure to be related to the variation in mean wages: *the ratio of emigrants from a particular region at a particular point in time to the total regional population before emigration.*

Thus, we follow a procedure that controls for all permanent differences in wage levels between regions and also for circumstances specific to particular years. Therefore, what effectively identifies the impact of emigration on wages is (solely) *the variation in the emigration share among regions and over time*, which is exactly the way theory suggests that changes in the supply of different types of labor should influence wages in regions. For regions, we use all 16 Polish *voivodeships* and for time, the years 1998-2007. The resulting data consist of 160 observations for each skill group.

Table 4: Descriptive Statistics

Variables	Mean	Std. Dev.	Variables	Mean	Std. Dev.
Non-emigrants			*Emigrants*		
			share of population	1.2%	1.0%
% female	51%	1%	% female	40%	11%
age	38.3	0.5	age	33.0	2.4
intermediate/low education	3.0	1.1	intermediate/low education	12.8	10.2
high/low education	0.7	0.3	high/low education	3.0	3.3
Net Wages			*Net Wages*		
log average	6.99	0.06	log average	6.95	0.34
log average low ed.	6.74	0.09	log average low ed.	6.40	1.72
log average intermediate ed.	6.94	0.59	log average intermediate ed.	6.55	1.45
log average high ed.	7.23	0.08	log average high ed.	6.62	1.39

Source: Polish LFS
Note: We report pooled means and standard deviations for all regions and years (1998 to 2007). Entries are the percentage of females, age, shares of individuals with intermediate and high levels of education divided by the share with low-level education, real net average wages, and real net wages by education group. For emigrants, we also report the share of emigrants out of the total working age population. The sample of emigrants we use to report wages is made up of the emigrants we observe before emigration and for whom we have labour market information. Real wages are stated in 2008 prices. Non-emigrants and emigrants are only those in the working age population (15-65).

This empirical strategy might fail if, for instance, regions that experience high international emigration also receive internal immigrants, as this could offset the effects of international emigration and lead to an under-estimation of the effect of emigration on wages. Likewise, if the same regions that experience high international emigration also experience emigration to other Polish regions, this could lead to an over-estimation of the effect of international emigration on regional wages. This is unlikely, because internal mobility in Poland across regions is low, and decreased over the period analysed.[3] Nevertheless, we performed several tests to check whether internal migration is correlated with international emigration, and found no evidence of this.

3.1 Non-random emigration

A particular source of concern is the possibility that *emigrants* are not a random sample of the regional population within each skill group. If migrants within an education group are positively (negatively) selected, then average wages for Polish residents in that education group could decrease (increase) after emigration purely as a result of a composition effect. Suppose, for example, that it was mostly the low-waged individuals from a given skill group who left Poland. That would contribute to a positive correlation between outflow and higher average wages for those members of that skill group who stayed in Poland – not because the wages of any individual workers staying in Poland increased, but solely because the wages of the more productive and higher-waged workers composed a larger share of the average wage for those who stayed.

We use a sub-sample of 857 emigrants for whom we have pre-emigration wage data to study whether they tend to be positively or negatively selected relative to non-emigrants. Our results indicate that there are no statistically significant differences in unobserved 'ability' between emigrants and non-emigrants, and hence that emigrants are not a biased sample of the resident population.

A further potential problem with our basic approach is that *emigration choices* may not be random. That is, although we account for permanent regional differences – and therefore also for the fact that, for instance, emigration may be higher from rural or traditionally less wealthy regions – it remains the case that even after these differences are controlled for, region-specific shocks affecting the wages of a given skill group in a given year could be correlated with regional emigration flows in the same year. Therefore, our basic approach – the standard *ordinary least squares* (OLS) estimator – could be biased. However, that potential bias would be downward. If, as seems plausible, emigration is higher from regions that experience negative wage shocks, then this association may induce a spurious negative correlation between emigration and wage growth that would lead to a negative bias in the estimate of the effect of emigration on mean wages. Hence, the results produced so far provide a lower bound for the actual effect of emigration on mean wages, and thus the actual effect might have been even higher, but not lower.

Even though we consider that we have established that our estimated results provide a lower bound for the actual effect of emigration on residents' wages, we

---

3 For instance, in 2001, 0.24% of the population reported living in a different region than in the previous year, and this share decreased to 0.12% in 2007.

also use another method of estimation to make sure that we have identified the causal effect of emigration on wages. To use this method we need something that influences emigration, but it should be uncorrelated with conditions in a particular Polish region. Here we use economic shocks, measured as real wage growth or GDP growth, to the main destination countries of Polish emigrants (Gemany, Ireland, the UK and the U.S.). These shocks should influence emigration and should not be correlated with shocks to a particular Polish region. We allow the effect of these shocks on the probability of migration to differ across regions through regional heterogeneity in migration costs to each potential destination country, and model this heterogeneity in several alternative ways.

4. Results

In Table 5, we report our estimated effect of emigration on average wages (row 1) and for the wages of the different education groups (rows 2 to 4). Panel A reports our baseline results, while panels B-D report different robustness checks. Column (1) reports the results from a specification that controls only for regional-specific effects and year-specific effects, while column (2) reports results when controls are added in for the size of the regional population, the average age in the region, and the educational and gender composition. All regressions refer to the years between 1998 and 2007. In panel A, we use net wages, as reported in the survey. The estimates in row 1 show that emigration is associated with a higher growth in regional average wages: the estimated coefficients range are 0.97 in column (1) and 1 in column (2), and are statistically significant in both cases at the 10% level. Because the variation used for estimation is the change in the stock of emigrants between consecutive years, these are short-run estimates. As pointed out in Section 2.2, a positive overall effect of emigration is compatible with the elasticity of capital supply not being infinite, at least in the short run. In terms of magnitude, the estimates in columns (2) imply that an increase of one percentage point in the ratio of emigrants to the total population led to a 1% increase in average real wages. Over the period considered, emigration from Poland increased on average by 0.19 percentage points per year and real wages increased by about 1.7% per year. These estimates therefore suggest that emigration may have contributed about 1/10 of the overall real wage growth.

Table 5: Effects of emigration on log mean wages

	A		B		C		D	
	Net wages		Gross wages		Imputed wages		Adjusting for single households	
	(1)	(2)	(3)	(4)	(5)	(6)	(7)	(8)
average	0.969*	0.999*	1.058*	1.100*	0.65	0.860*	0.903*	0.897*
	(0.551)	(0.558)	(0.590)	(0.596)	(0.519)	(0.518)	(0.481)	(0.532)
low	-1.154	-2.138	-1.664	-2.762	-1.243	-2.023	-1.684	-2.570*
	(1.510)	(1.463)	(1.783)	(1.728)	(1.336)	(1.287)	(1.329)	(1.386)
intermediate	1.285**	1.403**	1.463**	1.619***	1.033*	1.201**	1.047**	1.148**
	(0.569)	(0.569)	(0.619)	(0.614)	(0.559)	(0.562)	(0.493)	(0.547)
high	1.515*	1.142	1.647*	1.254	1.247*	1.037	1.903**	1.527*
	(0.861)	(0.871)	(0.906)	(0.918)	(0.671)	(0.684)	(0.751)	(0.824)
Region fixed effects	Yes	Yes	Yes	Yes	Yes	Yes	Yes	Yes
Year dummies	Yes	Yes	Yes	Yes	Yes	Yes	Yes	Yes
Other controls	No	Yes	No	Yes	No	Yes	No	Yes
Observations	160	160	160	160	160	160	160	160

Note: Entries are OLS-estimated regression coefficients of the ratio of emigrants to the total population on log average net wages and on log average wages by education groups for the years 1998-2007. In each panel we use a different measure of average, low, intermediate and high wages. In Panel A we use net monthly wages, as reported in the survey. In Panel B we reconstruct gross wages. In Panel C we impute wages for individuals who report being employed but do not report wages. In Panel D we adjust the share of emigrants by the share of single households in the population. All regressions include regional fixed effects. 'Other controls' are log regional population, mean regional age and gender, shares of people with intermediate and high levels of education compared to those with low levels of education. Newey-West standard errors using 1 lag are reported in parentheses. * indicates significance at 10%, ** at 5%, and *** at 1% levels.

In rows 2-4 of Table 5, we report the results for the three different education level groups. The figures in Table 2 suggest that emigration was mainly concentrated in the middle part of the educational distribution and far less at the bottom. As discussed in Section 2.2, the effect of emigration should thus be felt most by those with intermediate education, because this group experiences the largest (negative) relative supply shock. The results in rows 2-4 of Table 5 are in line with these predictions, suggesting that emigration led to an increase in wages for workers with an intermediate or high level of education but possibly depressed wages for those with a low level of education. The estimates for the low-education group are, however, not significantly different from zero.

Overall, these results conform remarkably well with the predictions of the simple model outlined in Section 2.2, with larger gains for workers in the skill categories exposed to a larger negative supply shock. They also indicate that emigration helped overall wage growth in Poland over the period under consideration, although it may have reduced returns to capital.

Panels B, C and D of Table 5 show that these results are robust to the use of gross, instead of net, wages as the dependent variable (panel B), to corrections for non-response to the wage question in the PLFS (panel C), and to the potential under-estimation of emigrant numbers due to single emigrant households not being captured in our data (panel D).

As we noted above, the estimates in Table 5 could form a lower bound for the actual effect of emigration on wages of non-residents. For this reason, we have also performed some estimations that factor out the possible effect of non-random emigration. Overall, the results of these additional estimations confirm the pattern shown in Table 5: workers in the intermediate skills category, who experienced the largest negative supply shock, have gained most in terms of wages. On the other hand, there was far less emigration by those in the lowest educational category, an observation with which the negative estimates obtained are compatible.

5. Discussion and Conclusions

We use the Polish Labour Force Survey (PLFS) to assess the effect that emigration had on the wages of Polish workers who did not emigrate over the period 1998-2007, which saw much outward migration from the country. The PLFS is unique in two respects: first, it asks households about household members who have migrated, which allows direct measurement of the migrant population; and second, it provides information about the emigrants' key characteristics, including age and educational level. We use this data to construct region- and skill-specific emigration rates.

Our basic results suggest that the large emigration experienced by Poland over the 1998-2007 period (when the emigrant share of the total population increased from 0.5 to 2.3%, and in some regions to up to 5.6%) contributed to overall wage growth by accounting for 1/10 of the growth in real wages – particularly for workers in the intermediate skill group, which experienced the largest negative labour supply shock. Our basic specification regresses variation in skill group-specific wage rates on region-specific emigration rates, conditioning on the age of emigrants, the educational composition of the sample and region-specific effects. Although these region-specific estimates are potentially biased by the fact that emigration may have been greater in regions that experienced negative shocks, the bias is likely to be downwards, allowing us to interpret our results as lower bounds.

To investigate this issue further, we implement an additional estimation strategy based on labour market shocks to the various destination countries. Our basic results from these exercises are very similar to the results of our basic estimations and re-confirm a slight overall positive effect on wages of emigration, with individuals in the intermediate-education group gaining most. Workers with intermediate-level education experienced at least an additional 0.25% real wage increase per year between 1998 and 2007 due to emigration. These results are robust to various checks on the definition of the wage variables – in which we account for missing information and for the effects of the fiscal system – and on the potential mismeasurement of regional emigration rates.

The effect on the highly educated is likewise positive, but a little smaller; an annual wage growth of 0.22% due to emigration is found in our study. The effect on the wages of those with a low level of education is slightly negative, albeit not significantly different from zero for most cases.

These effects should be compared to the overall wage growth for the groups studied: between 1998 and 2007, the average annual real wage growth was 1.3%, 1.4%, and 1.2% per year for workers with low, intermediate, and high levels of education respectively.[4]

Taken together, our findings suggest that emigration from Poland over the 1998-2007 period had a positive (although not always precisely estimated) effect on the average wages of those who did not emigrate. Our results are thus in line with those that Aydemir and Borjas (2007) and Mishra (2007) find, using a different empirical strategy, for Mexican emigration. Moreover, the impact of migration on wages for the different skill groups seems to mirror the relative negative supply shocks experienced by these skill groups through emigration; that is, the emigrants were drawn primarily from the medium and upper parts of the educational distribution, in which positive wage effects are more pronounced. Not everyone gained, however: according to our point estimates, workers with a low level of education – the group that emigrated least and thus became relatively more abundant in Poland – experienced no wage gains and may even have experienced slight wage decreases.

---

4 Note that the average annual growth rates for each education group are lower than the growth rate of average wages. This can happen because the relative size of education groups changed considerably between 1998 and 2007.

References

Aydemir, Abdurrahman and George J. Borjas. 2007. 'Cross-Country Variation in the Impact of International Migration: Canada, Mexico, and the United States'. *Journal of the European Economic Association*, 5(4), 663-708.

Dustmann, Christian, Tommaso Frattini, and Ian Preston (2012). 'The Effect of Immigration along the Distribution of Wages'. *Review of Economics Studies* (forthcoming).

Fassmann, Heinz and Rainer Munz (1994). 'European East-West Migration, 1945-1992'. *International Migration Review*, 28(3), 520-538.

Kaczmarczyk, Paweł and Marek Okólski (2008). 'Demographic and Labour-Market Impacts of Migration on Poland'. *Oxford Review of Economic Policy*, 24(3), 599-624.

Kaczmarczyk, Paweł, Marta Mioduszewska, and Anna Zylicz (2009). 'Impact of the Post-Accession Migration on the Polish Labour Market'. In *EU Enlargement and the Labor Markets: What Do We Know?*, edited by Martin Kahanec and Klaus F. Zimmermann. Springer-Verlag Berlin, pp. 219-253.

Mishra, Prachi (2007). 'Emigration and Wages in Source Countries: Evidence from Mexico'. *Journal of Development Economics*, 82(1), 180-199.

Zubrzycki, Jerzy (1953). 'Emigration from Poland in the Nineteenth and Twentieth Centuries'. *Population Studies*, 6(3), 248-272.